Give your brain a boost with CGP!

Pencils at the ready — this fantastic book from CGP is going to take pupils' Mental Maths skills from zero to hero in no time at all.

It's bursting with activities designed to build those crucial Mental Maths skills, with every single day of the spring term covered.

We also included heaps of helpful examples and engaging pictures to aid pupils along the way. Ideal for use anywhere — at home, in class, on a rollercoaster...

What CGP is all about

Our sole aim here at CGP is to produce the highest quality books
— carefully written, immaculately presented and
dangerously close to being funny.

Then we work our socks off to get them out to you
— at the cheapest possible prices.

Contents

☑ Use the tick boxes to help keep a record of which tests have been attempted.

Week 1
- ☑ Day 1 1
- ☑ Day 2 2
- ☑ Day 3 3
- ☑ Day 4 4
- ☑ Day 5 5

Week 2
- ☑ Day 1 6
- ☑ Day 2 7
- ☑ Day 3 8
- ☑ Day 4 9
- ☑ Day 5 10

Week 3
- ☑ Day 1 11
- ☑ Day 2 12
- ☑ Day 3 13
- ☑ Day 4 14
- ☑ Day 5 15

Week 4
- ☑ Day 1 16
- ☑ Day 2 17
- ☑ Day 3 18
- ☑ Day 4 19
- ☑ Day 5 20

Week 5
- ☑ Day 1 21
- ☑ Day 2 22
- ☑ Day 3 23
- ☑ Day 4 24
- ☑ Day 5 25

Week 6
- ☑ Day 1 26
- ☑ Day 2 27
- ☑ Day 3 28
- ☑ Day 4 29
- ☑ Day 5 30

Week 7
- ☑ Day 1 31
- ☑ Day 2 32
- ☑ Day 3 33
- ☑ Day 4 34
- ☑ Day 5 35

Week 8
- ☑ Day 1 36
- ☑ Day 2 37
- ☑ Day 3 38
- ☑ Day 4 39
- ☑ Day 5 40

Week 9

- [✓] Day 1 41
- [✓] Day 2 42
- [✓] Day 3 43
- [✓] Day 4 44
- [✓] Day 5 45

Week 10

- [✓] Day 1 46
- [✓] Day 2 47
- [✓] Day 3 48
- [✓] Day 4 49
- [✓] Day 5 50

Week 11

- [✓] Day 1 51
- [✓] Day 2 52
- [✓] Day 3 53
- [✓] Day 4 54
- [✓] Day 5 55

Week 12

- [✓] Day 1 56
- [✓] Day 2 57
- [✓] Day 3 58
- [✓] Day 4 59
- [✓] Day 5 60

Answers 61

Published by CGP

ISBN: 978 1 78908 764 2

Editors: Emma Clayton, Charlotte Sheridan, Hayley Thompson

With thanks to Emma Wright and George Wright for the proofreading.

With thanks to Emily Smith for the copyright research.

Cover and graphics used throughout the book © www.edu-clips.com
Clipart from Corel®

Coin images used on pages 1, 14, 29 and 45: 5 and 50 pence coins © iStock.com/duncan1890, 10 pence coins © iStock.com/john shepherd, 20 pence coins © iStock.com/Jaap2, 2 pence coins © iStock.com/peterspiro, 1 pence coins © iStock.com/coopder1

Printed by W&G Baird Ltd, Antrim.
Based on the classic CGP style created by Richard Parsons.

Text, design, layout and original illustrations © Coordination Group Publications Ltd. (CGP) 2021
All rights reserved.

Photocopying this book is not permitted, even if you have a CLA licence.
Extra copies are available from CGP with next day delivery • 0800 1712 712 • www.cgpbooks.co.uk

How to Use this Book

- This book contains 60 daily practice tests.

- We've split them into 12 sections — that's roughly one for each week of the Year 2 spring term.

- Each week is made up of 5 tests, so there's one for every school day of the term (Monday – Friday).

- Each test should take about 10 minutes to complete.

- Pupils should aim to do their working in their heads, without writing it down.

- The tests contain a mix of mental maths topics from Year 2. New Year 2 topics are gradually introduced as you go through the book.

- The tests increase in difficulty as you progress through the term.

- Each test looks something like this:

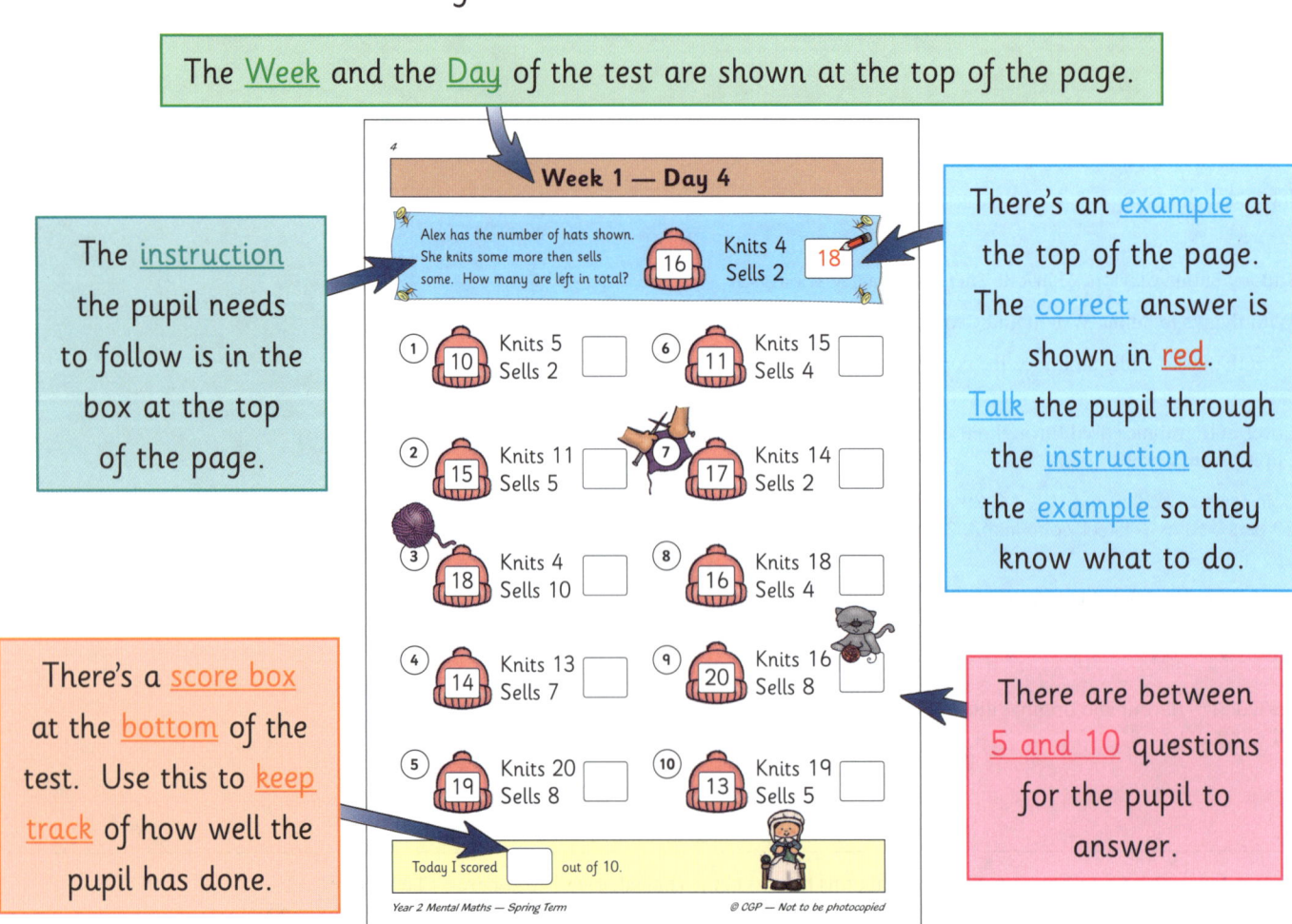

Week 1 — Day 1

Do the coins add up to the amount shown? Circle yes or no.  13p yes /(no)

1. 25p yes / no

5.  82p yes / no

2.  44p yes / no

6.  37p yes / no

3.  19p yes / no

7.  71p yes / no

4.  33p yes / no

8.  79p yes / no

Today I scored ☐ out of 8.

© CGP — Not to be photocopied   Year 2 Mental Maths — Spring Term

Week 1 — Day 2

What is the total number of sides on the shapes?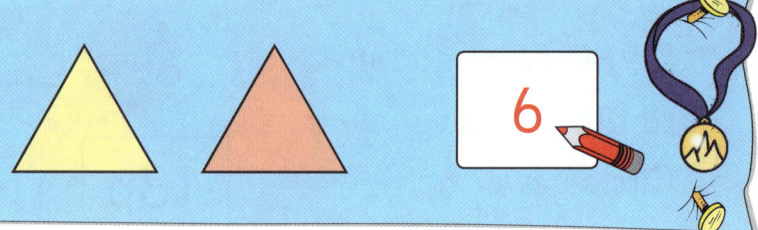

1.
2.
3.
4.
5.

6.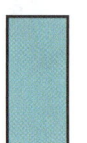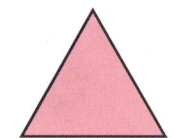
7.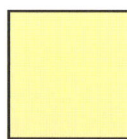
8.
9.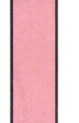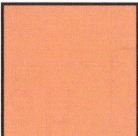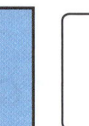
10.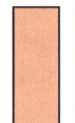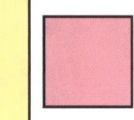

Today I scored ☐ out of 10.

Year 2 Mental Maths — Spring Term

Week 1 — Day 3

Look at the subtraction in the pink box. Fill in the missing number to show a sum you could do to check the answer.

19 − 5 = 14

14 + **5**

1) 12 − 9 = 3

3 + ☐

2) 38 − 20 = 18

18 + ☐

3) 76 − 67 = 9

☐ + 9

4) 92 − 85 = 7

☐ + 85

5) 47 − 36 = 11

☐ + 36

6) 22 − 12 = 10

12 + ☐

7) 59 − 43 = 16

16 + ☐

8) 63 − 58 = 5

☐ + 5

Today I scored ☐ out of 8.

Week 1 — Day 4

Alex has the number of hats shown. She knits some more then sells some. How many are left in total?  16 Knits 4 Sells 2  18

1.  10 Knits 5 Sells 2

2.  15 Knits 11 Sells 5

3.  18 Knits 4 Sells 10

4.  14 Knits 13 Sells 7

5.  19 Knits 20 Sells 8

6.  11 Knits 15 Sells 4

7.  17 Knits 14 Sells 2

8.  16 Knits 18 Sells 4

9.  20 Knits 16 Sells 8

10.  13 Knits 19 Sells 5

Today I scored ☐ out of 10.

Year 2 Mental Maths — Spring Term

Week 1 — Day 5

Fill in the missing number.

40 + 15 = 55

1) 30 + ☐ = 44

6) 61 + ☐ = 91

2) ☐ + 88 = 98

7) 13 + 67 = ☐

3) 24 + 35 = ☐

8) 47 + ☐ = 54

4) ☐ + 71 = 87

9) 39 + ☐ = 51

5) 48 + 13 = ☐

10) ☐ + 74 = 92

Today I scored ☐ out of 10.

Week 2 — Day 1

Fill in the missing number. Wednesday is **2** days after Monday.

1) Thursday is ☐ days after Monday.

2) Tuesday is ☐ days after Sunday.

3) Friday is ☐ days before Monday.

4) Wednesday is ☐ days before Friday.

5) Sunday is ☐ days after Wednesday.

6) Monday is ☐ days after Saturday.

7) Thursday is ☐ days before Sunday.

8) Saturday is ☐ days before Tuesday.

9) Friday is ☐ days before Tuesday.

10) Wednesday is ☐ days after Saturday.

Today I scored ☐ out of 10.

Week 2 — Day 2

Circle all of the numbers that obey the rule.

The ones digit is a 3.

① The tens digit is a 6.

② The ones digit is one less than the tens digit.

③ The tens digit is half of the ones digit.

④ The ones digit is four times the tens digit.

⑤ The ones digit is greater than 5.
The tens digit is an odd number.

Today I scored ☐ out of 5.

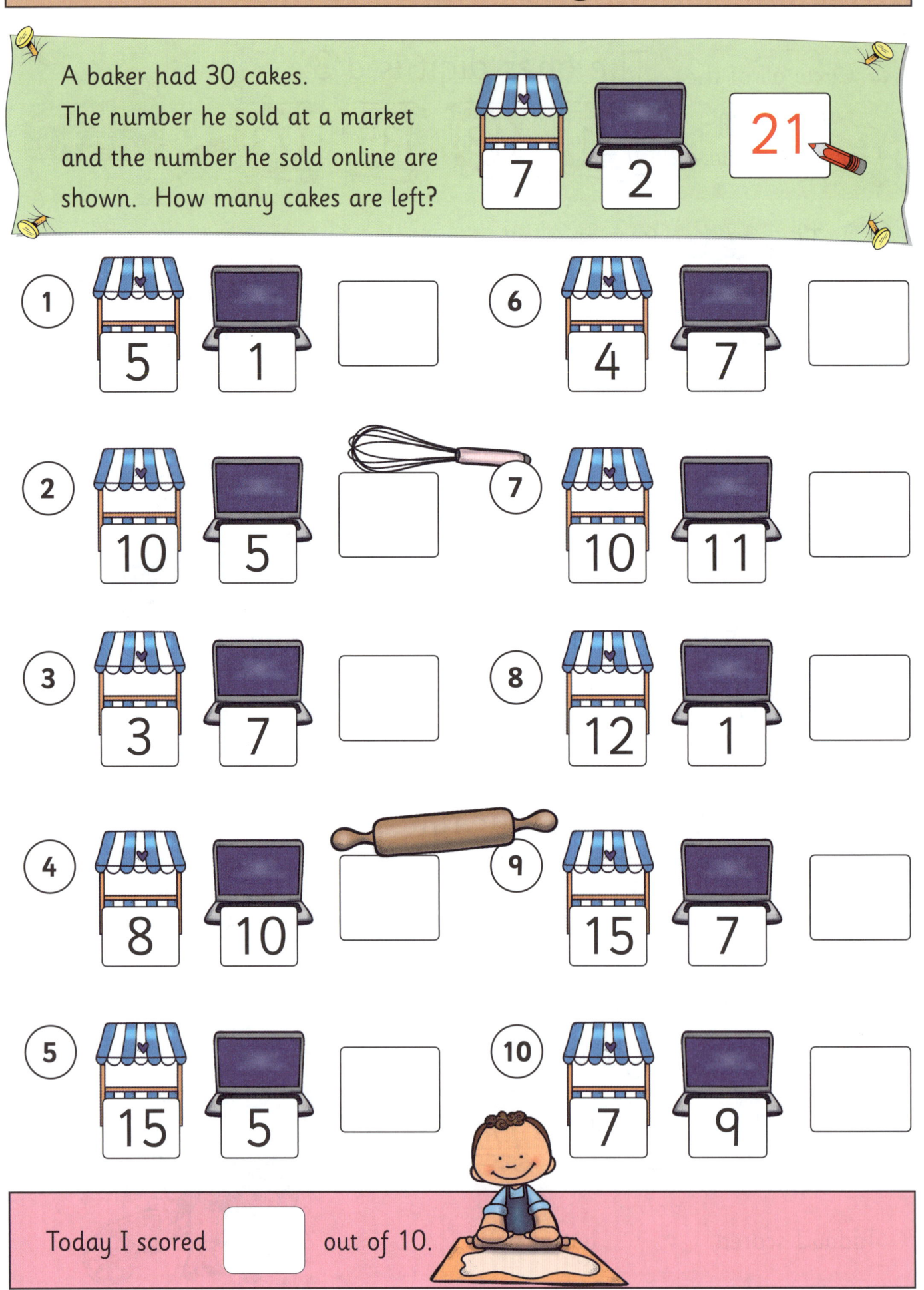

Week 2 — Day 4

Write a multiplication fact for the addition shown.

1) + = ☐ × ☐

2) + + + = ☐ × ☐

3) + + = ☐ × ☐

4) + = ☐ × ☐

5) + + + + + = ☐ × ☐

6) + + + + = ☐ × ☐

Today I scored ☐ out of 6.

Week 2 — Day 5

A library gives children a gold star every time they read 5 books. How many books did the children read to get their stars?

 3 stars — 15 books

1.  2 stars — ____ books

2.  10 stars — ____ books

3.  5 stars — ____ books

4.  4 stars — ____ books

5.  8 stars — ____ books

6.  11 stars — ____ books

7.  9 stars — ____ books

8.  12 stars — ____ books

Today I scored ____ out of 8.

Week 3 — Day 1

Circle the amount of the shape that is shaded. 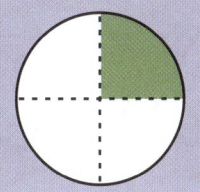 ~~one quarter~~ one whole one half

1. 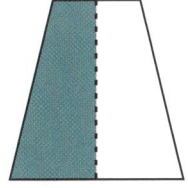 one quarter one whole one half

2. 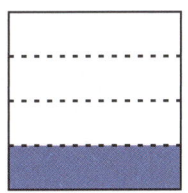 one quarter three quarters one half

3. 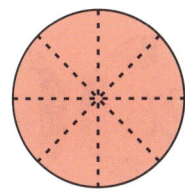 three quarters one whole one half

4.  three quarters one quarter one half

5. 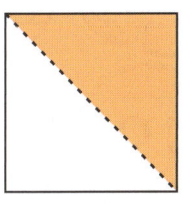 one quarter three quarters one half

6.  one quarter one whole one half

7. 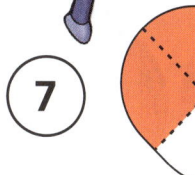 one quarter one half three quarters

8. 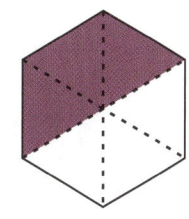 one quarter one whole one half

9. 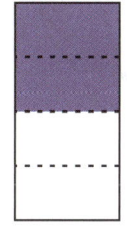 one quarter one whole two quarters

10. 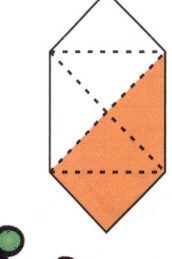 one quarter three quarters one half

Today I scored ☐ out of 10.

Week 3 — Day 3

What number is the child thinking of?  "If I multiply my number by 2, I get 16."

1) "If I multiply my number by 2, I get 20."

5) "If I multiply my number by 5, I get 25."

2) "If I multiply my number by 10, I get 40."

6) "If I multiply my number by 5, I get 45."

3) "If I multiply my number by 5, I get 15."

7) "If I multiply my number by 4, I get 20."

4) "If I multiply my number by 2, I get 12."

8) "If I multiply my number by 7, I get 14."

Today I scored ☐ out of 8.

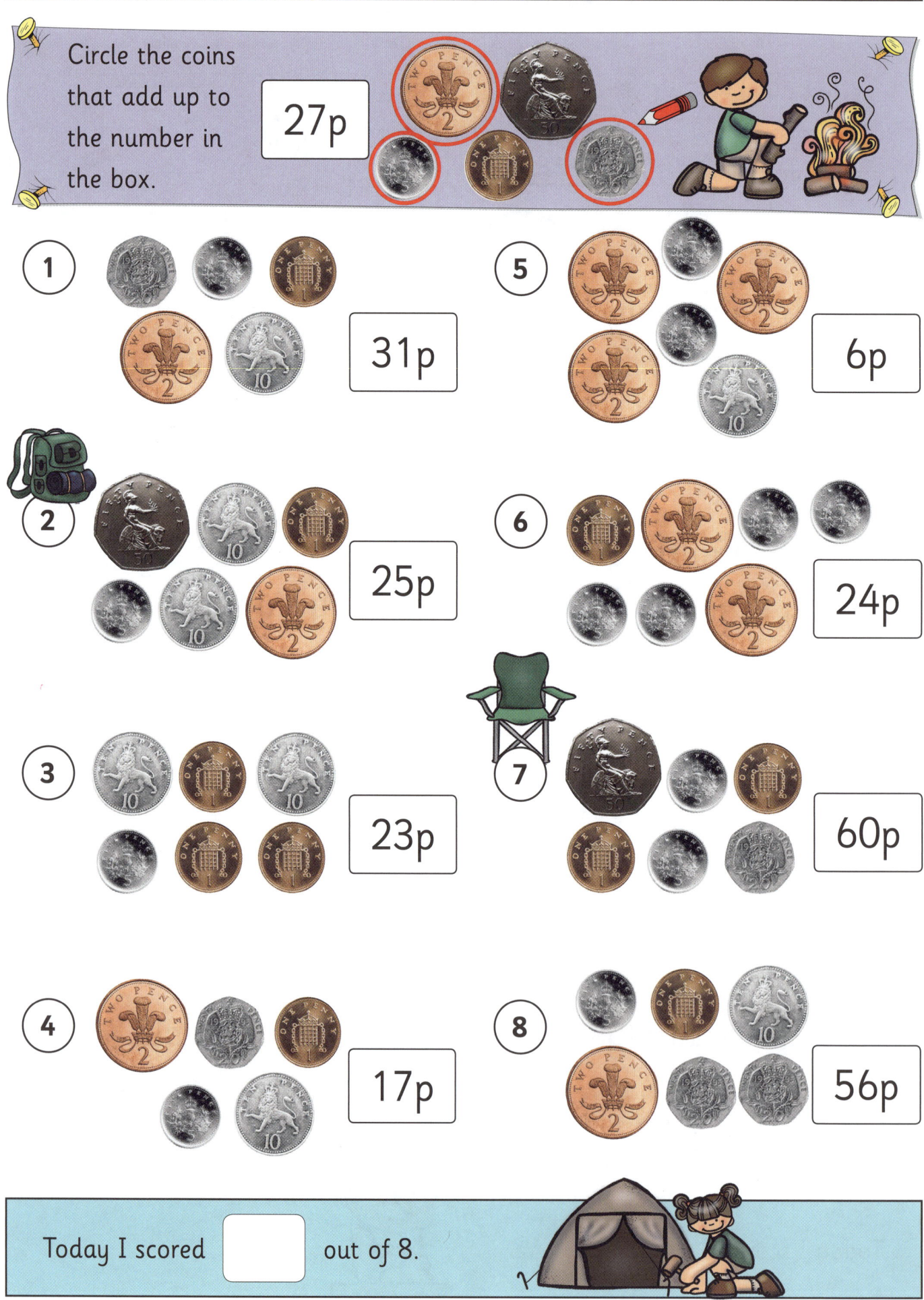

Week 3 — Day 5

Write <, > or = in the box.   2 × 6 < 9 + 5

1) 3 + 8 ☐ 5 × 2

2) 20 ÷ 5 ☐ 7 – 3

3) 16 – 8 ☐ 2 × 4

4) 7 × 2 ☐ 5 + 11

5) 50 ÷ 10 ☐ 3 × 2

6) 18 ÷ 2 ☐ 12 – 4

7) 3 × 10 ☐ 37 – 8

8) 9 – 6 ☐ 10 ÷ 5

9) 35 ÷ 7 ☐ 3 + 3

10) 5 × 6 ☐ 15 + 16

Today I scored ☐ out of 10.

Week 4 — Day 1

Write <, > or = in the box.   The length of the pencil [>] 3 cm.

1. The length of the pencil [ ] 6 cm.

2. The length of the pencil [ ] 4 cm.

3. The length of the pencil [ ] 10 cm.

4. The length of the pencil [ ] 9 cm.

5. The length of the pencil [ ] 25 cm.

6. The length of the pencil [ ] 35 cm.

Today I scored [ ] out of 6.

Week 4 — Day 2

Fill in the answer. | 8 | | 2 | | 5 | Add the centre number to the bottom number. | 7 |

1. | 10 | | 6 | | 7 | Add the top number to the bottom number.

2. | 2 | | 7 | | 4 | Multiply the top number by the centre number.

3. | 18 | | 13 | | 11 | Subtract the centre number from the top number.

4. | 5 | | 10 | | 20 | Divide the bottom number by the top number.

5. | 21 | | 17 | | 13 | Add the bottom number to the number above it.

6. | 15 | | 12 | | 20 | Subtract the centre number from the number below it.

Today I scored ☐ out of 6.

Week 4 — Day 3

Write down all the even numbers between the two numbers shown.

16 | 18   20 | 21

1) 4 _____ 10

2) 12 _____ 18

3) 21 _____ 26

4) 41 _____ 48

5) 32 _____ 39

6) 68 _____ 75

7) 17 _____ 23

8) 52 _____ 60

9) 24 _____ 33

10) 77 _____ 85

Today I scored ☐ out of 10.

Week 4 — Day 4

Work out the answer. $1 + 4 + 2 = \boxed{7}$

1) $5 + 2 + 2 =$ ☐

2) $7 + 3 + 4 =$ ☐

3) $6 + 6 + 1 =$ ☐

4) $3 + 8 + 3 =$ ☐

5) $4 + 9 + 7 =$ ☐

6) $7 + 5 + 4 =$ ☐

7) $1 + 7 + 9 =$ ☐

8) $2 + 5 + 8 =$ ☐

9) $9 + 2 + 7 =$ ☐

10) $5 + 9 + 8 =$ ☐

Today I scored ☐ out of 10.

Week 4 — Day 5

Work out the answer.   4 ÷ 2 = [2]

1) 10 ÷ 2 =

2) 20 ÷ 10 =

3) 6 ÷ 2 =

4) 15 ÷ 5 =

5) 40 ÷ 10 =

6) 25 ÷ 5 =

7) 18 ÷ 2 =

8) 14 ÷ 2 =

9) 40 ÷ 5 =

10) 24 ÷ 2 =

Today I scored [ ] out of 10.

Week 5 — Day 1

Circle the longer length. 20 cm (2 m)

1) 4 cm 40 cm

2) 17 m 35 m

3) 54 cm 40 cm

4) 3 m 3 cm

5) 15 cm 30 m

6) 9 cm 10 m

7) 4 m 5 cm

8) 2 m 88 cm

9) 1 m 90 cm

10) 200 cm 1 m

Today I scored ☐ out of 10.

Week 5 — Day 2

Use the multiplication in pink to help you write the answer to the division.

$5 \times 2 = 10$

$10 \div 2 = $ 5

1) $3 \times 5 = 15$
$15 \div 5 = $

2) $2 \times 4 = 8$
$8 \div 2 = $

3) $10 \times 3 = 30$
$30 \div 10 = $

4) $5 \times 10 = 50$
$50 \div 5 = $

5) $2 \times 8 = 16$
$16 \div 2 = $

6) $5 \times 4 = 20$
$20 \div 4 = $

7) $10 \times 6 = 60$
$60 \div 6 = $

8) $9 \times 2 = 18$
$18 \div 9 = $

9) $5 \times 9 = 45$
$45 \div 9 = $

10) $12 \times 2 = 24$
$24 \div 2 = $

Today I scored ☐ out of 10.

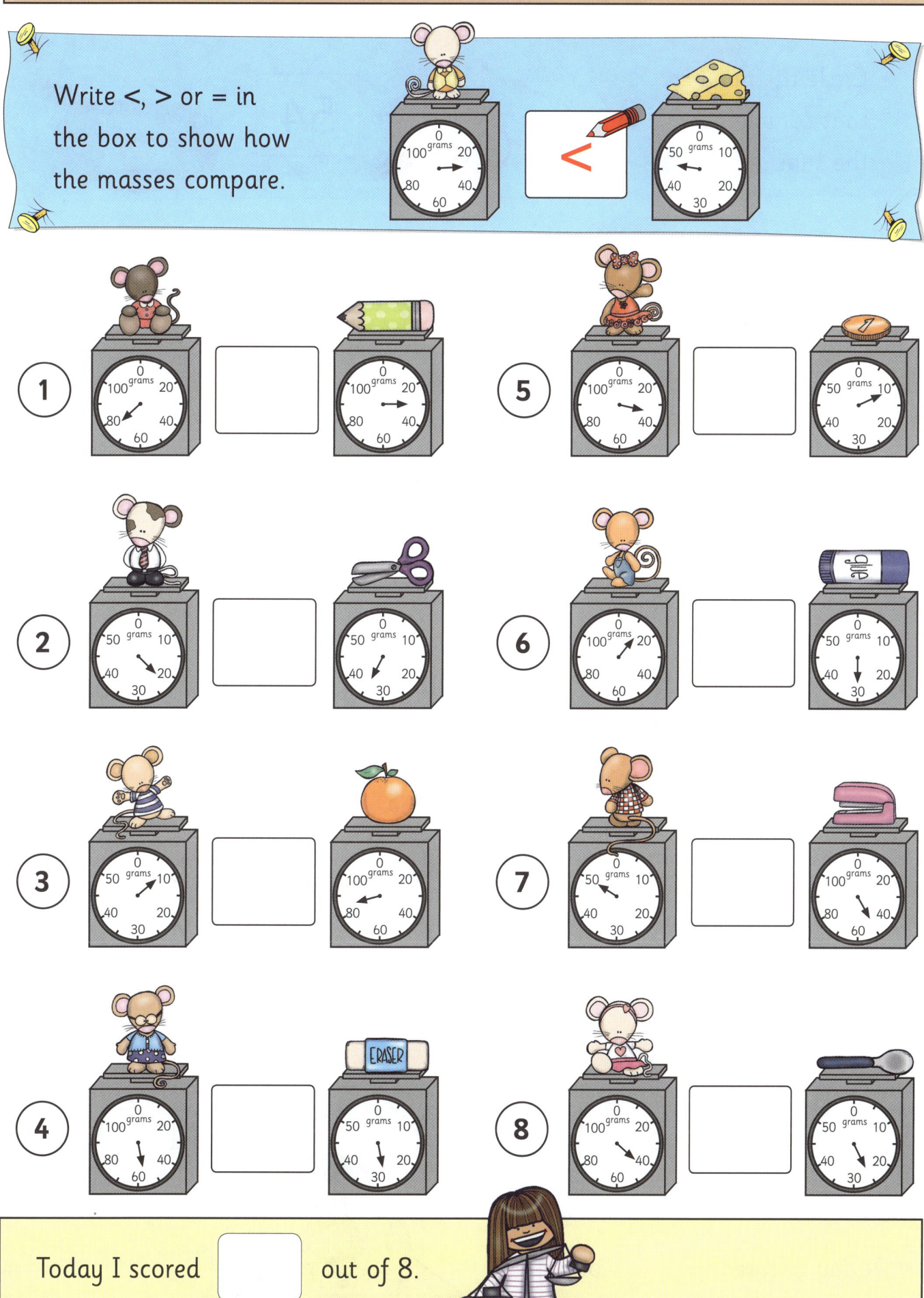

Week 5 — Day 4

Circle the number that completes the sum.

$34 + \begin{matrix} 12 \\ ⓩ⓪ \end{matrix} = 54$

1) $12 + \begin{matrix} 6 \\ 4 \end{matrix} = 18$

2) $56 + \begin{matrix} 26 \\ 10 \end{matrix} = 66$

3) $22 + \begin{matrix} 16 \\ 11 \end{matrix} = 38$

4) $51 + \begin{matrix} 19 \\ 22 \end{matrix} = 73$

5) $64 + \begin{matrix} 13 \\ 15 \end{matrix} = 79$

6) $74 + \begin{matrix} 13 \\ 17 \end{matrix} = 87$

7) $45 + \begin{matrix} 15 \\ 25 \end{matrix} = 60$

8) $19 + \begin{matrix} 12 \\ 14 \end{matrix} = 33$

9) $36 + \begin{matrix} 16 \\ 14 \end{matrix} = 52$

10) $58 + \begin{matrix} 24 \\ 34 \end{matrix} = 82$

Today I scored ☐ out of 10.

Week 6 — Day 1

Use the sum to complete the multiplication. Then write the answer.

2 + 2 = 2 × 2 = 4

1) 5 + 5 = ☐ × 5 = ☐

2) 2 + 2 + 2 = ☐ × 2 = ☐

3) 10 + 10 + 10 = ☐ × 10 = ☐

4) 5 + 5 + 5 + 5 = ☐ × 5 = ☐

5) 10 + 10 + 10 + 10 = ☐ × 10 = ☐

6) 2 + 2 + 2 + 2 + 2 = ☐ × 2 = ☐

7) 10 + 10 + 10 + 10 + 10 = ☐ × 10 = ☐

8) 5 + 5 + 5 + 5 + 5 + 5 + 5 = ☐ × 5 = ☐

Today I scored ☐ out of 8.

Week 6 — Day 2

Work out the answer.   29 − 11 = 18

1) 55 − 10 =

2) 47 − 8 =

3) 78 − 16 =

4) 96 − 9 =

5) 23 − 12 =

6) 88 − 24 =

7) 31 − 21 =

8) 64 − 33 =

9) 45 − 16 =

10) 74 − 26 =

Today I scored ☐ out of 10.

Week 6 — Day 3

The house numbers on a street go up in steps of 3. Fill in the missing house numbers.

21 | 24 | 27 | 30

1) 9, __, 15, __, 21, 24

2) 45, 48, 51, __, __, 60

3) 27, __, 33, 36, 39, __

4) 52, 55, __, __, 64, 67

5) __, 29, __, 35, 38, 41

Today I scored ☐ out of 5.

Week 6 — Day 4

Lily has the coins shown. How much more money does she need to buy the treat? 81p

11p

1. 32p — __ p
2. 16p — __ p
3. 40p — __ p
4. 95p — __ p
5. 19p — __ p
6. 48p — __ p
7. 30p — __ p
8. 52p — __ p

Today I scored ___ out of 8.

Week 6 — Day 5

Some blue marbles and red marbles are added to an empty bag. How many marbles are in the bag in total?

11 + 33 → **44**

1) 20 + 17 →
2) 41 + 22 →
3) 13 + 36 →
4) 38 + 42 →
5) 25 + 16 →
6) 59 + 12 →
7) 17 + 65 →
8) 28 + 28 →
9) 47 + 39 →
10) 48 + 43 →

Today I scored ☐ out of 10.

Week 7 — Day 1

Put the masses in order. Start with the heaviest.

| 34 kg | 53 kg | 12 kg |

| 53 kg | 34 kg | 12 kg |

1) 43 kg   78 kg   20 kg   33 kg   56 kg

___ kg   ___ kg   ___ kg   ___ kg   ___ kg

2) 16 kg   89 kg   90 kg   37 kg   45 kg

___ kg   ___ kg   ___ kg   ___ kg   ___ kg

3) 27 kg   11 kg   22 kg   68 kg   70 kg

___ kg   ___ kg   ___ kg   ___ kg   ___ kg

4) 49 kg   94 kg   41 kg   55 kg   57 kg

___ kg   ___ kg   ___ kg   ___ kg   ___ kg

5) 62 kg   15 kg   46 kg   19 kg   64 kg

___ kg   ___ kg   ___ kg   ___ kg   ___ kg

Today I scored ___ out of 5.

Week 7 — Day 2

Write the answer as a word. 10 ÷ 5 = [two]

1) 4 ÷ 2 =

2) 30 ÷ 10 =

3) 20 ÷ 2 =

4) 8 ÷ 2 =

5) 60 ÷ 5 =

6) 70 ÷ 10 =

7) 12 ÷ 2 =

8) 5 ÷ 5 =

9) 30 ÷ 6 =

10) 18 ÷ 2 =

Today I scored [ ] out of 10.

Week 7 — Day 3

Fill in the missing numbers in the table.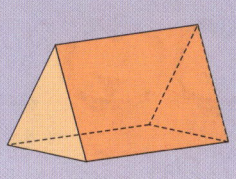

Faces	Edges	Vertices
5	9	6

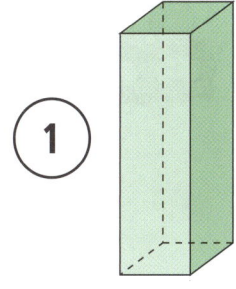

1)

Faces	Edges	Vertices
		8

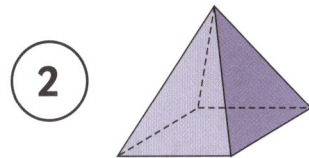

2)

Faces	Edges	Vertices
5		

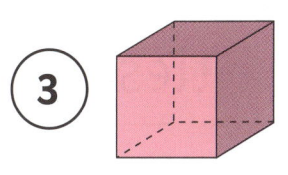

3)

Faces	Edges	Vertices
	12	

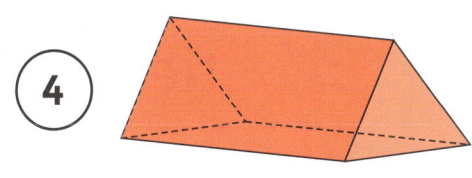

4)

Faces	Edges	Vertices
		6

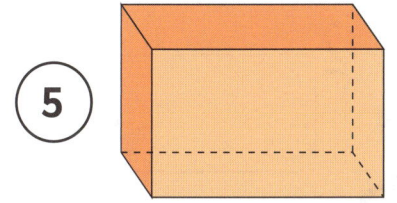

5)

Faces	Edges	Vertices
6		

Today I scored ☐ out of 5.

Week 7 — Day 4

Each vampire has 2 capes and 5 ties. How many capes and ties do the vampires have in total?

3 vampires — **6** capes, **15** ties

1. 2 vampires — [ ] capes [ ] ties
2. 5 vampires — [ ] capes [ ] ties
3. 4 vampires — [ ] capes [ ] ties
4. 7 vampires — [ ] capes [ ] ties
5. 9 vampires — [ ] capes [ ] ties

Today I scored [ ] out of 5.

Week 7 — Day 5

Circle the pair of numbers that add up to the number in the star.

1)

6)

2)

7)

3)

8)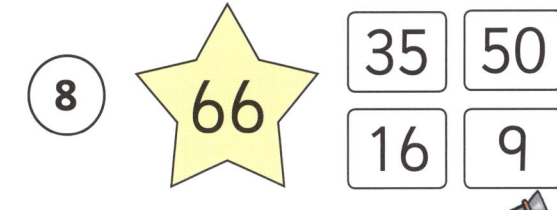

4)

9)

5)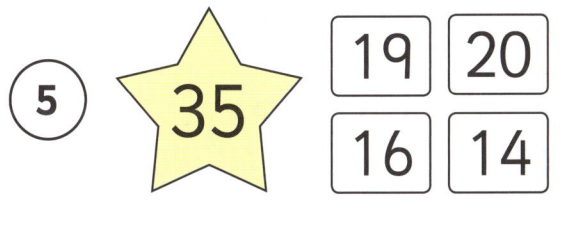

10)

Today I scored ☐ out of 10.

Week 8 — Day 1

A golfer shares golf balls equally between the people in her lesson. How balls many does each person get?

6 balls
3 people

2

1) 50 balls
10 people

2) 50 balls
5 people

3) 10 balls
2 people

4) 20 balls
5 people

5) 10 balls
10 people

6) 20 balls
10 people

7) 20 balls
2 people

8) 20 balls
4 people

9) 15 balls
3 people

10) 14 balls
7 people

Today I scored ☐ out of 10.

Week 8 — Day 3

How many suitcases is the luggage truck pulling in total?

1) 8, 9, 3 — suitcases

6) 52, 39 — suitcases

2) 7, 4, 5 — suitcases

7) 47, 25 — suitcases

3) 14, 20 — suitcases

8) 29, 27 — suitcases

4) 27, 32 — suitcases

9) 36, 48 — suitcases

5) 35, 45 — suitcases

10) 39, 53 — suitcases

Today I scored ☐ out of 10.

Week 8 — Day 4

The tally chart shows some people's favourite thing about spring.
Use this tally chart and the sentence given to answer the question.

Favourite	lambs	daffodils	sunshine
Tally	𝍷𝍷𝍷𝍷𝍷 𝍷𝍷𝍷	𝍷𝍷𝍷𝍷	𝍷𝍷𝍷𝍷𝍷 𝍷

12 more people liked calves than lambs.
How many people liked calves? **20**

1) 12 more people liked tulips than daffodils.
How many people liked tulips? ☐

2) 14 more people liked ducklings than lambs.
How many people liked ducklings? ☐

3) 13 more people liked rainbows than sunshine.
How many people liked rainbows? ☐

4) 3 fewer people liked bluebells than daffodils.
How many people liked bluebells? ☐

5) 6 fewer people liked tadpoles than lambs.
How many people liked tadpoles? ☐

Today I scored ☐ out of 5.

Week 8 — Day 5

A beach bucket holds 5 l of water.
A drinks bottle holds 2 l of water.
Write < or > in the box.

4 full buckets hold [<] 25 l

1) 2 full buckets hold [ ] 12 l

2) 3 full bottles hold [ ] 9 l

3) 7 full bottles hold [ ] 10 l

4) 3 full buckets hold [ ] 14 l

5) 10 full buckets hold [ ] 20 l

6) 11 full bottles hold [ ] 25 l

7) 5 full buckets hold [ ] 22 l

8) 8 full bottles hold [ ] 18 l

Today I scored [ ] out of 8.

Week 9 — Day 1

Tick the difference in time between the two clocks.

	quarter of an hour	half an hour	an hour
	✓		
1			
2			
3			
4			
5			
6			

Today I scored [ ] out of 6.

Week 9 — Day 2

Fill in the missing number.　2 × 7 = 14

1) ☐ ÷ 2 = 5

2) ☐ ÷ 5 = 9

3) 3 × 10 = ☐

4) 7 × 5 = ☐

5) ☐ ÷ 5 = 10

6) ☐ ÷ 2 = 8

7) ☐ ÷ 10 = 7

8) 5 × 5 = ☐

9) 9 × 10 = ☐

10) ☐ ÷ 5 = 6

Today I scored ☐ out of 10.

Week 9 — Day 3

Circle the number sentence that gives the bigger total.   ⬭ 27 + 20 ⬭   67 − 30

1) 23 + 20   62 − 10
2) 19 + 10   38 − 10
3) 14 + 50   79 − 30
4) 43 + 20   87 − 30
5) 36 + 40   99 − 20
6) 55 + 10   86 − 30
7) 62 + 20   98 − 30
8) 52 + 40   85 − 20

Today I scored ☐ out of 8.

Week 9 — Day 4

The pictogram shows how many people play each instrument.

Instrument	Number of People
Saxophone	☐☐☐
Piano	☐☐☐☐☐
Double Bass	☐☐

Key: ☐ = 2 people

How many people play the piano? **10**

1.

Instrument	Number of People
Drums	☐☐☐
Horn	☐☐☐☐
Harp	☐

How many people play the drums? ☐

2.

Instrument	Number of People
Cornet	☐
Tuba	☐
Harmonica	☐☐☐

How many people play the tuba? ☐

3.

Instrument	Number of People
Guitar	☐☐☐☐
Singing	☐☐
Triangle	☐☐☐☐

How many people sing? ☐

4.

Instrument	Number of People
Clarinet	☐☐
Trombone	☐☐
Cymbals	☐

How many people play the cymbals? ☐

5.

Instrument	Number of People
Flute	☐☐☐☐☐
Recorder	☐☐☐☐☐☐
Xylophone	☐☐☐

How many people play the flute? ☐

6.

Instrument	Number of People
Cello	☐☐☐☐
Violin	☐☐
Trumpet	☐☐

How many people the play the cello? ☐

Today I scored ☐ out of 6.

Week 10 — Day 1

Circle the two numbers that add to make 40.

1) 20 10
   15 30

2) 5 35
   27 10

3) 20 17
   13 23

4) 16 4
   26 14

5) 9 21
   39 31

6) 11 21
   29 9

7) 29 33
   7 1

8) 1 39
   11 9

9) 36 24
   4 6

10) 16 24
    4 26

Today I scored ☐ out of 10.

Week 10 — Day 2

Circle the number sentences with an even answer. Cross the number sentences with an odd answer.

1) | 10 + 8 | 10 + 7 |

2) | 10 − 5 | 10 − 6 |

3) | 12 + 6 | 12 + 7 |

4) | 19 − 7 | 19 − 10 |

5) | 35 + 8 | 35 + 6 |

6) | 23 − 6 | 23 + 7 |

7) | 42 + 8 | 42 + 6 |

8) | 19 + 9 | 19 − 9 |

Today I scored ☐ out of 8.

Week 10 — Day 3

Use the blue number cards to make two different calculations that add up to the number given.

5 3 2

5 2 + 1 3 = 65

5 3 + 1 2 = 65

0 3 2

1) 2 ☐ + ☐ ☐ = 52

2 ☐ + ☐ ☐ = 52

3 2 1

4) 4 ☐ + ☐ ☐ = 73

4 ☐ + ☐ ☐ = 73

5 3 4

2) 6 ☐ + ☐ ☐ = 99

6 ☐ + ☐ ☐ = 99

4 1 3

5) 4 ☐ + ☐ ☐ = 57

4 ☐ + ☐ ☐ = 57

1 4 2

3) 2 ☐ + ☐ ☐ = 36

2 ☐ + ☐ ☐ = 36

7 1 5

6) 2 ☐ + ☐ ☐ = 42

2 ☐ + ☐ ☐ = 42

Today I scored ☐ out of 6.

Week 10 — Day 4

Tick 'Yes' or 'No' to say if you can swap the numbers in the number sentence and get the same answer.

4 + 5 Yes ✓ No ☐

1) 14 ÷ 2   Yes ☐ No ☐
2) 8 − 3   Yes ☐ No ☐
3) 3 × 4   Yes ☐ No ☐
4) 2 + 6   Yes ☐ No ☐
5) 20 ÷ 5   Yes ☐ No ☐
6) 5 × 10   Yes ☐ No ☐
7) 9 − 4   Yes ☐ No ☐
8) 7 − 2   Yes ☐ No ☐
9) 5 + 3   Yes ☐ No ☐
10) 2 × 6   Yes ☐ No ☐

Today I scored ☐ out of 10.

Week 10 — Day 5

The block diagram shows how many cans, bottles and cardboard boxes were recycled by Class 2C.

What is the difference in 'number recycled' for the objects given?

bottles and cans **3**

1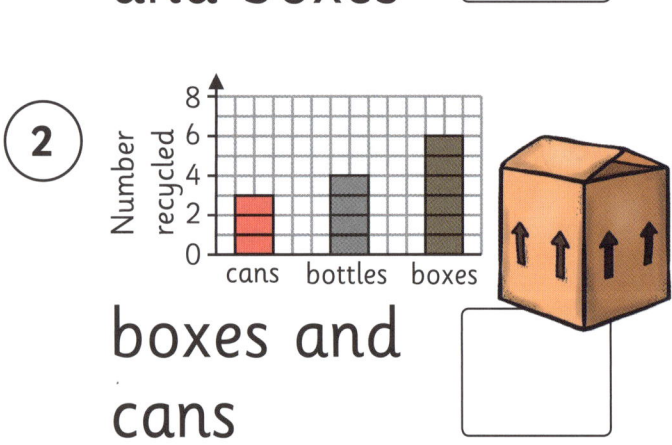

bottles and boxes ☐

2

boxes and cans ☐

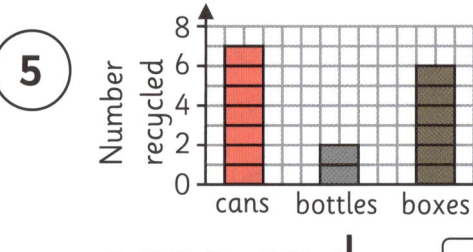

3

cans and bottles ☐

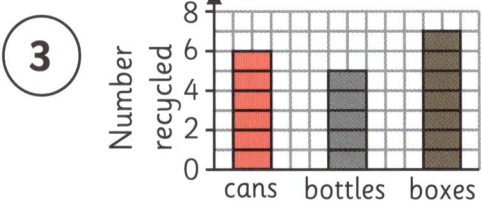

4

bottles and boxes ☐

5

cans and bottles ☐

6

boxes and cans ☐

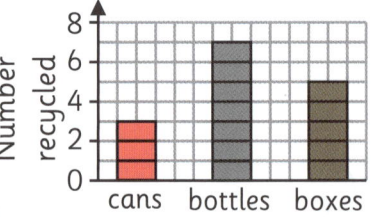

Today I scored ☐ out of 6.

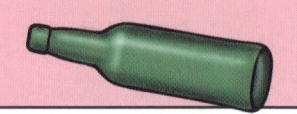

Week 11 — Day 1

Look at the theatre clock and ticket. Tick the box if the time shown on the clock is before the show start time. Cross the box if it is after.

1

5

2

6

3

7

4

8

Today I scored [ ] out of 8.

Week 11 — Day 2

Work out the answer.   23 + 16 = 39

1) 29 + 30 =
2) 36 + 25 =
3) 27 + 71 =
4) 17 + 37 =
5) 16 + 12 =
6) 25 + 56 =
7) 37 + 26 =
8) 19 + 25 =
9) 36 + 52 =
10) 12 + 29 =

Today I scored [ ] out of 10.

Week 11 — Day 3

Use the repeated addition fact to complete the division.

5 + 5 = 10

10 ÷ 5 = 2

1) 2 + 2 + 2 = 6   ☐ ÷ 2 = ☐

2) 5 + 5 + 5 = 15   ☐ ÷ 5 = ☐

3) 10 + 10 = 20   ☐ ÷ 10 = ☐

4) 2 + 2 + 2 + 2 = 8   ☐ ÷ 2 = ☐

5) 10 + 10 + 10 + 10 = 40   ☐ ÷ 10 = ☐

6) 2 + 2 + 2 + 2 + 2 = 10   ☐ ÷ 2 = ☐

7) 5 + 5 + 5 + 5 = 20   ☐ ÷ 5 = ☐

Today I scored ☐ out of 7.

Week 12 — Day 1

Write ÷ or × to complete the number sentence.   2 × 4 = 8

1) 2 ☐ 2 = 4

2) 6 ☐ 2 = 3

3) 10 ☐ 2 = 5

4) 16 ☐ 2 = 8

5) 4 ☐ 5 = 20

6) 12 ☐ 2 = 24

7) 6 ☐ 2 = 12

8) 22 ☐ 2 = 11

9) 9 ☐ 2 = 18

10) 15 ☐ 3 = 5

Today I scored ☐ out of 10.

Week 12 — Day 2

Look at the objects. How many of the 3D shapes have the same number of faces? **2**

1.

2.

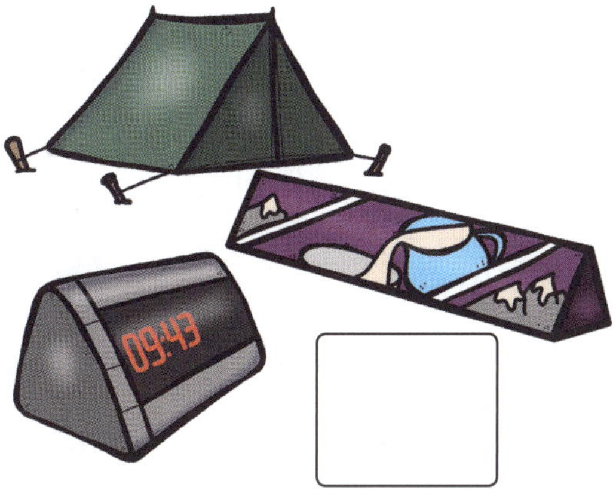

3.

4.

5.

6.

Today I scored ☐ out of 6.

Week 12 — Day 3

Circle the two numbers that multiply together to make the number in the target.

1)

2)

3)

4)

5)

6)

7)

8)

Today I scored 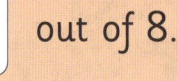 out of 8.

Week 12 — Day 4

Circle the amounts that add up to the cost of the item in the cafe.

29p   (4p)   (20p)   (5p)   23p

1. 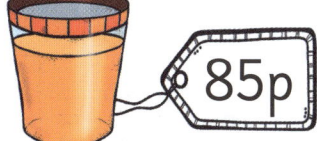 85p | 40p | 42p | 60p | 25p |

2.  30p | 2p | 3p | 20p | 25p |

3.  35p | 15p | 30p | 20p | 10p |

4.  55p | 20p | 45p | 40p | 10p |

5.  80p | 10p | 5p | 50p | 20p |

6.  89p | 5p | 6p | 4p | 80p |

7.  99p | 59p | 40p | 30p | 50p |

8.  45p | 39p | 29p | 16p | 7p |

Today I scored ☐ out of 8.

Week 12 — Day 5

Fill in the missing number.   8 + 1 = 16 − 7

1) 2 + 3 = 20 − ☐

2) 11 + ☐ = 20 − 8

3) 2 + 1 = 10 − ☐

4) 13 + 2 = 25 − ☐

5) 5 + ☐ = 25 − 14

6) 7 + 3 = 17 − ☐

7) 3 + ☐ = 15 − 10

8) 15 + 5 = 30 − ☐

9) 12 + 8 = 32 − ☐

10) 7 + ☐ = 37 − 20

Today I scored ☐ out of 10.

Answers

Week 1 — Day 1
1. yes
2. no
3. no
4. yes
5. no
6. yes
7. yes
8. no

Week 1 — Day 2
1. 8
2. 7
3. 12
4. 7
5. 9
6. 11
7. 12
8. 10
9. 16
10. 15

Week 1 — Day 3
1. 9
2. 20
3. 67
4. 7
5. 11
6. 10
7. 43
8. 58

Week 1 — Day 4
1. 13
2. 21
3. 12
4. 20
5. 31
6. 22
7. 29
8. 30
9. 28
10. 27

Week 1 — Day 5
1. 14
2. 10
3. 59
4. 16
5. 61
6. 30
7. 80
8. 7
9. 12
10. 18

Week 2 — Day 1
1. 3
2. 2
3. 3
4. 2
5. 4
6. 2
7. 3
8. 3
9. 4
10. 4

Week 2 — Day 2
1. 62, 69
2. 98, 54
3. 36, 12, 48
4. 14, 28
5. 17, 79, 36

Week 2 — Day 3
1. 24
2. 15
3. 20
4. 12
5. 10
6. 19
7. 9
8. 17
9. 8
10. 14

Week 2 — Day 4
1. 2 × 5
2. 4 × 2
3. 3 × 5
4. 2 × 10
5. 6 × 2
6. 5 × 5

Week 2 — Day 5
1. 10
2. 50
3. 25
4. 20
5. 40
6. 55
7. 45
8. 60

Week 3 — Day 1
1. one half
2. one quarter
3. one whole
4. one quarter
5. one half
6. one half
7. three quarters
8. one half
9. two quarters
10. one half

Week 3 — Day 2
1. even numbers: 32, 50, 14
   10 times table: 50
2. even numbers: 4, 60
   10 times table: 60
3. even numbers: 34, 30, 20
   10 times table: 30, 20
4. even numbers: 30, 46, 22, 36
   10 times table: 30
5. even numbers: 26, 40, 44
   10 times table: 40
6. even numbers: 46, 70, 52, 60
   10 times table: 70, 60

Week 3 — Day 3
1. 10
2. 4
3. 3
4. 6
5. 5
6. 9
7. 5
8. 2

Week 3 — Day 4
1. 20p, 10p, 1p
2. 10p, 10p, 5p
3. 10p, 10p, 1p, 1p, 1p
4. 10p, 5p, 2p
5. 2p, 2p, 2p
6. 5p, 5p, 5p, 5p, 2p, 2p
7. 50p, 5p, 5p
8. 20p, 20p, 10p, 5p, 1p

Week 3 — Day 5
1. >
2. =
3. =
4. <
5. <
6. >
7. >
8. >
9. <
10. <

Week 4 — Day 1
1. <
2. =
3. >
4. <
5. =
6. <

Week 4 — Day 2
1. 17
2. 14
3. 5
4. 4
5. 30
6. 8

Week 4 — Day 3
1. 6, 8
2. 14, 16
3. 22, 24
4. 42, 44, 46
5. 34, 36, 38
6. 70, 72, 74
7. 18, 20, 22
8. 54, 56, 58
9. 26, 28, 30, 32
10. 78, 80, 82, 84

Week 4 — Day 4
1. 9
2. 14
3. 13
4. 14
5. 20
6. 16
7. 17
8. 15
9. 18
10. 22

Week 4 — Day 5
1. 5
2. 2
3. 3
4. 3
5. 4
6. 5
7. 9
8. 7
9. 8
10. 12

Week 5 — Day 1
1. 40 cm
2. 35 m
3. 54 cm
4. 3 m
5. 30 m
6. 10 m
7. 4 m
8. 2 m
9. 1 m
10. 200 cm

Week 5 — Day 2
1. 3
2. 4
3. 3
4. 10
5. 8
6. 5
7. 10
8. 2
9. 5
10. 12

Week 5 — Day 3
1. >
2. <
3. <
4. >
5. >
6. <
7. =
8. >

Week 5 — Day 4
1. 6
2. 10
3. 16
4. 22
5. 15
6. 13
7. 15
8. 14
9. 16
10. 24

Week 5 — Day 5
1. 9
2. 8
3. 17
4. 12
5. 19

Week 6 — Day 1
1. **2 × 5 = 10**
2. **3 × 2 = 6**
3. **3 × 10 = 30**
4. **4 × 5 = 20**
5. **4 × 10 = 40**
6. **5 × 2 = 10**
7. **5 × 10 = 50**
8. **7 × 5 = 35**

Week 6 — Day 2
1. 45
2. 39
3. 62
4. 87
5. 11
6. 64
7. 10
8. 31
9. 29
10. 48

Week 6 — Day 3
1. 12, 18
2. 54, 57
3. 30, 42
4. 58, 61
5. 26, 32

Week 6 — Day 4
1. 2p
2. 5p
3. 8p
4. 15p
5. 11p
6. 13p
7. 12p
8. 7p

Week 6 — Day 5
1. 37
2. 63
3. 49
4. 80
5. 41
6. 71
7. 82
8. 56
9. 86
10. 91

Week 7 — Day 1

1. 78 kg, 56 kg, 43 kg, 33 kg, 20 kg
2. 90 kg, 89 kg, 45 kg, 37 kg, 16 kg
3. 70 kg, 68 kg, 27 kg, 22 kg, 11 kg
4. 94 kg, 57 kg, 55 kg, 49 kg, 41 kg
5. 64 kg, 62 kg, 46 kg, 19 kg, 15 kg

Week 7 — Day 2

1. two
2. three
3. ten
4. four
5. twelve
6. seven
7. six
8. one
9. five
10. nine

Week 7 — Day 3

1. faces: 6
   edges: 12
2. edges: 8
   vertices: 5
3. faces: 6
   vertices: 8
4. faces: 5
   edges: 9
5. edges: 12
   vertices: 8

Week 7 — Day 4

1. 4 capes, 10 ties
2. 10 capes, 25 ties
3. 8 capes, 20 ties
4. 14 capes, 35 ties
5. 18 capes, 45 ties

Week 7 — Day 5

1. 10, 30
2. 16, 13
3. 22, 35
4. 33, 17
5. 19, 16
6. 20, 27
7. 80, 13
8. 50, 16
9. 52, 32
10. 35, 35

Week 8 — Day 1

1. 5
2. 10
3. 5
4. 4
5. 1
6. 2
7. 10
8. 5
9. 5
10. 2

Week 8 — Day 2

1. 4
2. 3
3. 4
4. 8
5. 5
6. 6
7. 6
8. 6

Week 8 — Day 3

1. 20
2. 16
3. 34
4. 59
5. 80
6. 91
7. 72
8. 56
9. 84
10. 92

Week 8 — Day 4

1. 16
2. 22
3. 19
4. 1
5. 2

Week 8 — Day 5

1. <
2. <
3. >
4. >
5. >
6. <
7. >
8. <

Week 9 — Day 1

1. an hour
2. an hour
3. quarter of an hour
4. half an hour
5. quarter of an hour
6. an hour

Week 9 — Day 2

1. 10
2. 45
3. 30
4. 35
5. 50
6. 16
7. 70
8. 25
9. 90
10. 30

Week 9 — Day 3

1. 62 − 10
2. 19 + 10
3. 14 + 50
4. 43 + 20
5. 99 − 20
6. 55 + 10
7. 62 + 20
8. 52 + 40

Week 9 — Day 4

1. 6
2. 2
3. 3
4. 1
5. 9
6. 7

Week 9 — Day 5

1. 1p
2. 2p
3. 10p
4. 5p
5. 50p
6. 10p
7. 2p
8. 50p

Week 10 — Day 1
1. 10, 30
2. 5, 35
3. 17, 23
4. 26, 14
5. 31, 9
6. 29, 11
7. 33, 7
8. 39, 1
9. 36, 4
10. 16, 24

Week 10 — Day 2
1. (10 + 8), ~~10 + 7~~
2. ~~10 – 5~~, (10 – 6)
3. (12 + 6), ~~12 + 7~~
4. (19 – 7), ~~19 – 10~~
5. ~~35 + 8~~, (35 + 6)
6. ~~23 – 6~~, (23 + 7)
7. (42 + 8), (42 + 6)
8. (19 + 9), (19 – 9)

Week 10 — Day 3
1. **20** + **32** = 52
   22 + **30** = 52
2. 6**5** + **34** = 99
   6**4** + **35** = 99
3. **24** + **12** = 36
   22 + **14** = 36
4. **42** + **31** = 73
   4**1** + **32** = 73
5. **43** + **14** = 57
   4**4** + **13** = 57
6. **27** + **15** = 42
   25 + **17** = 42

Week 10 — Day 4
1. No
2. No
3. Yes
4. Yes
5. No
6. Yes
7. No
8. No
9. Yes
10. Yes

Week 10 — Day 5
1. 1
2. 3
3. 1
4. 3
5. 5
6. 2

Week 11 — Day 1
1. ✓
2. ✓
3. ✗
4. ✓
5. ✗
6. ✓
7. ✗
8. ✗

Week 11 — Day 2
1. 59
2. 61
3. 98
4. 54
5. 28
6. 81
7. 63
8. 44
9. 88
10. 41

Week 11 — Day 3
1. **6** ÷ 2 = **3**
2. **15** ÷ 5 = **3**
3. **20** ÷ 10 = **2**
4. **8** ÷ 2 = **4**
5. **40** ÷ 10 = **4**
6. **10** ÷ 2 = **5**
7. **20** ÷ 5 = **4**

Week 11 — Day 4
1. 10 °C
2. 20 °C
3. 5 °C
4. 7 °C
5. 22 °C
6. 17 °C

Week 11 — Day 5
1. 20
2. 9
3. 80
4. 12
5. 30
6. 19
7. 16
8. 33

Week 12 — Day 1
1. ×
2. ÷
3. ÷
4. ÷
5. ×
6. ×
7. ×
8. ÷
9. ×
10. ÷

Week 12 — Day 2
1. 2
2. 2
3. 3
4. 0
5. 3
6. 3

Week 12 — Day 3
1. 6, 2
2. 3, 5
3. 2, 4
4. 1, 10
5. 2, 7
6. 10, 9
7. 5, 8
8. 5, 12

Week 12 — Day 4
1. 60p, 25p
2. 2p, 3p, 25p
3. 15p, 20p
4. 45p, 10p
5. 50p, 20p, 10p
6. 5p, 4p, 80p
7. 59p, 40p
8. 16p, 29p

Week 12 — Day 5
1. 15
2. 1
3. 7
4. 10
5. 6
6. 7
7. 2
8. 10
9. 12
10. 10

Answers